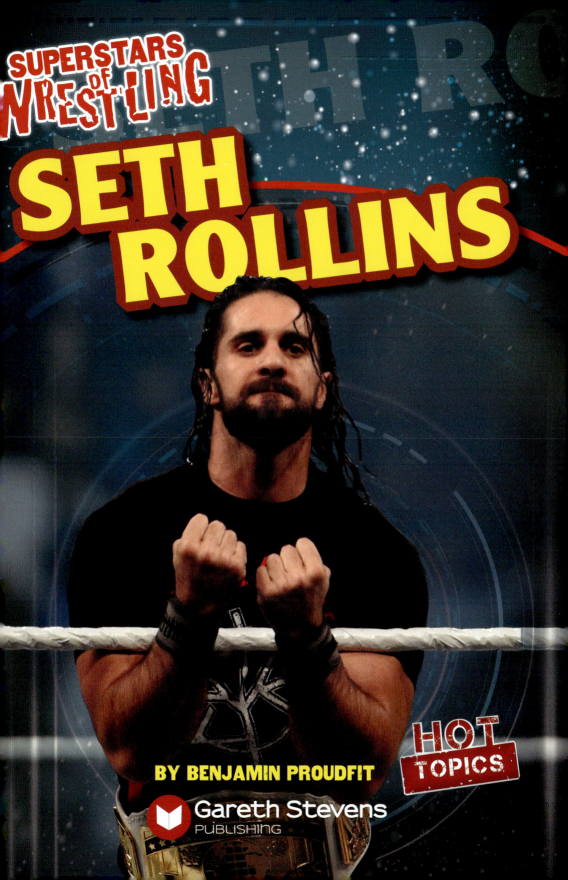

Please visit our website, www.garethstevens.com. For a free color catalog of all our high-quality books, call toll free 1-800-542-2595 or fax 1-877-542-2596.

Library of Congress Cataloging-in-Publication Data

Names: Proudfit, Benjamin, author.
Title: Seth Rollins / Benjamin Proudfit.
Description: New York : Gareth Stevens Publishing, 2022. | Series: Superstars of wrestling | Includes index.
Identifiers: LCCN 2020032275 (print) | LCCN 2020032276 (ebook) | ISBN 9781538266038 (library binding) | ISBN 9781538266014 (paperback) | ISBN 9781538266021 (set) | ISBN 9781538266045 (ebook)
Subjects: LCSH: Rollins, Seth, 1986---Juvenile literature. | World Wrestling Entertainment, Inc.--Biography--Juvenile literature. | Wrestlers--United States--Biography--Juvenile literature.
Classification: LCC GV1196.R655 P76 2022 (print) | LCC GV1196.R655 (ebook) | DDC 796.812092 [B]--dc23
LC record available at https://lccn.loc.gov/2020032275
LC ebook record available at https://lccn.loc.gov/2020032276

First Edition

Published in 2022 by
Gareth Stevens Publishing
29 E. 21st Street
New York, NY 10010

Copyright © 2022 Gareth Stevens Publishing

Designer: Michael Flynn
Editor: Kristen Nelson

Photo credits: Cover, pp. 1, 5, 27 (Lesnar) Fayez Nureldine/AFP/Getty Images; p. 7 https://commons.wikimedia.org/wiki/File:Jimmy_Jacobs_and_Tyler_Black.jpg; pp. 9, 21 JP Yim/Getty Images; pp. 11, 25 Sylvain Lefevre/Getty Images; p. 13 https://commons.wikimedia.org/wiki/File:WWE_2014-05-22_22-35-17_ILCE-6000_2342_DxO_(14125149259).jpg; p. 15 https://commons.wikimedia.org/wiki/File:WWE_Raw_IMG_5895_(13773018875).jpg; p. 17 Marc Pfitzenreuter/Getty Images; p. 19 https://en.wikipedia.org/wiki/Seth_Rollins#/media/File:Seth_Rollins_holds_Money_in_the_Bank_briefcase_at_a_WWE_house_show_in_January_2015.jpg; p. 23 Jim Spellman/Getty Images; p. 27 (Rollins) Etsuo Hara/Getty Images; p. 29 Kevin Mazur/Getty Images.

All rights reserved. No part of this book may be reproduced in any form without permission in writing from the publisher, except by a reviewer.

Printed in the United States of America

CPSIA compliance information: Batch #CSGS22: For further information contact Gareth Stevens, New York, New York at 1-800-542-2595.

CONTENTS

Born to Wrestle — 4

Indie Start — 6

NXT Time — 10

The Shield — 12

A Big First — 14

Going Solo — 16

Out and Back — 20

WrestleMania Run — 22

Seth's Future — 28

The Best of Seth Rollins — 30

For More Information — 31

Glossary — 32

Index — 32

BORN TO WRESTLE

Seth Rollins is one of the top wrestlers in World Wrestling Entertainment (WWE) today. He was born Colby Lopez on May 28, 1986, in Iowa. Seth found a love for wrestling as a teenager. He and his friends put on backyard wrestling shows!

IN THE RING

Seth started training as a wrestler after he finished high school in 2004. He drove three hours to get to the wrestling school!

INDIE START

Seth had his first **matches** in 2005. He worked for **independent** companies, including Pro Wrestling Guerrilla (PWG) in California. By 2007, he'd begun wrestling for Ring of Honor (ROH). There, he wrestled under the name Tyler Black.

IN THE RING

Seth's first in-ring name was Gixx.

7

In ROH, Seth won the tag team titles with Jimmy Jacobs. In February 2010, he won the ROH World Championship too. He lost the title in September after signing with the WWE. His in-ring name soon became Seth Rollins.

IN THE RING

Florida Championship Wrestling (FCW) was part of WWE's **developmental** program. There, Seth won the tag team titles and the FCW Florida Heavyweight Championship.

NXT TIME

FCW's name changed to NXT in 2012. Seth **debuted** on NXT's TV show in June. By the end of August, he'd won an eight-man **tournament** and become the first-ever NXT Champion! That was just the beginning for Seth in WWE.

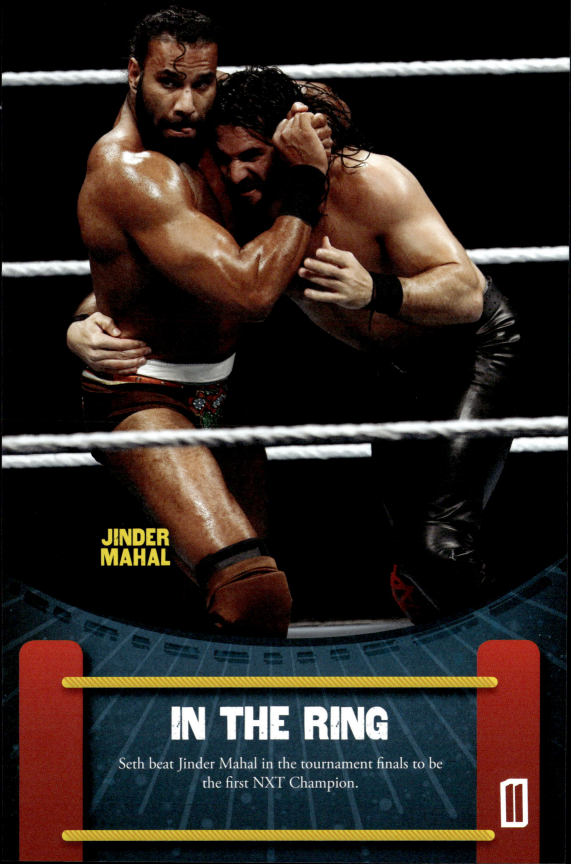

THE SHIELD

Just a few months later, Seth made his **main roster** debut at Survivor Series. He, Roman Reigns, and Dean Ambrose entered through the crowd as The Shield. Their first match as a **stable** was at TLC in December 2012 against Daniel Bryan, Kane, and Ryback.

IN THE RING

The Shield started as heels, or bad guys. Their job was to help WWE superstar CM Punk.

A BIG FIRST

The Shield made waves in WWE, winning matches and showing great in-ring skill. They faced Randy Orton, the Big Show, and Sheamus at WrestleMania 29 in April 2013. It was the first WrestleMania match for all three members of The Shield—and they won!

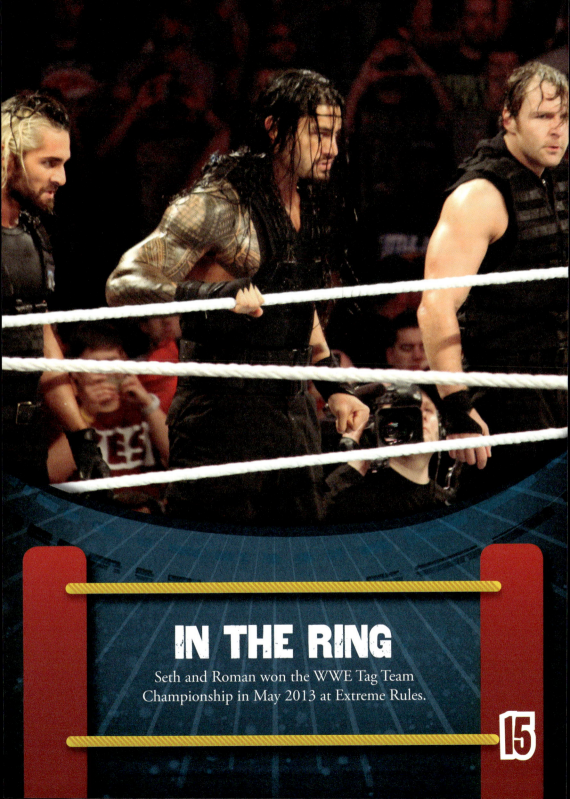

IN THE RING

Seth and Roman won the WWE Tag Team Championship in May 2013 at Extreme Rules.

15

GOING SOLO

At WrestleMania 30, The Shield again won their match. Soon after, they began a **feud** with Triple H. They took on Triple H and Evolution, beating them at both Extreme Rules and Payback. But in June 2014, Seth turned on The Shield.

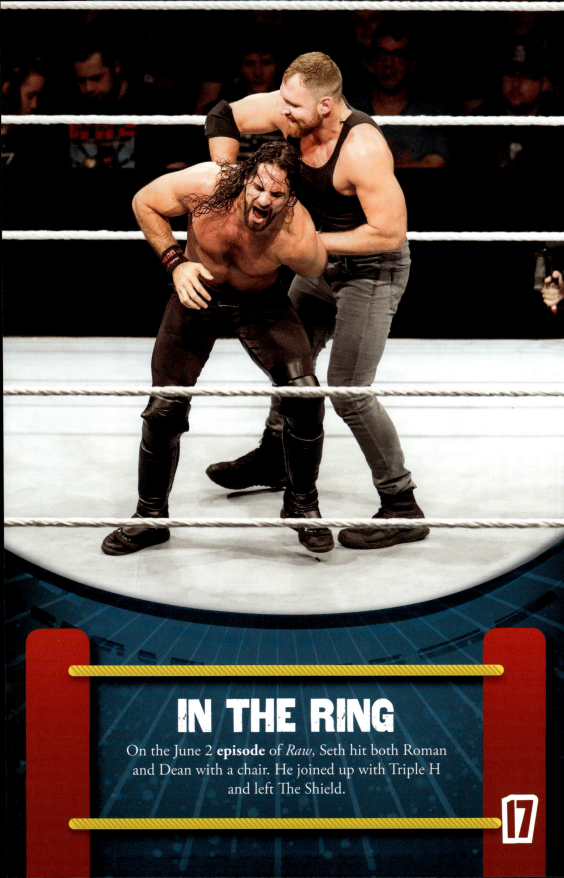

IN THE RING

On the June 2 **episode** of *Raw*, Seth hit both Roman and Dean with a chair. He joined up with Triple H and left The Shield.

Seth was ready to become a solo star. He won the Money in the Bank ladder match in June 2014 and cashed in the briefcase at WrestleMania 31 in March 2015. He beat Brock Lesnar and Roman Reigns for the WWE World Heavyweight title!

IN THE RING

Seth won the United States Championship from John Cena at SummerSlam 2015. He held two titles at once!

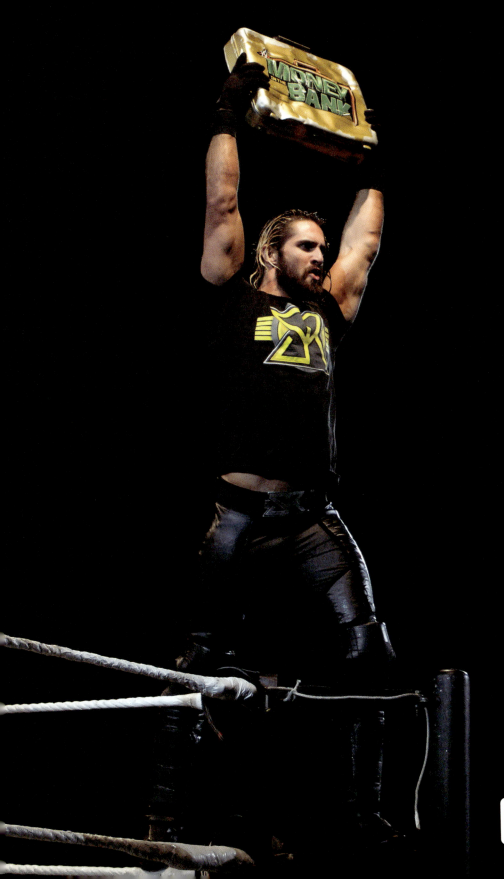

OUT AND BACK

Seth was WWE champion until November 2015. He badly hurt his knee and had to give up the title. Seth worked hard to come back to the ring in May 2016. He feuded with Roman Reigns for the championship—and won!

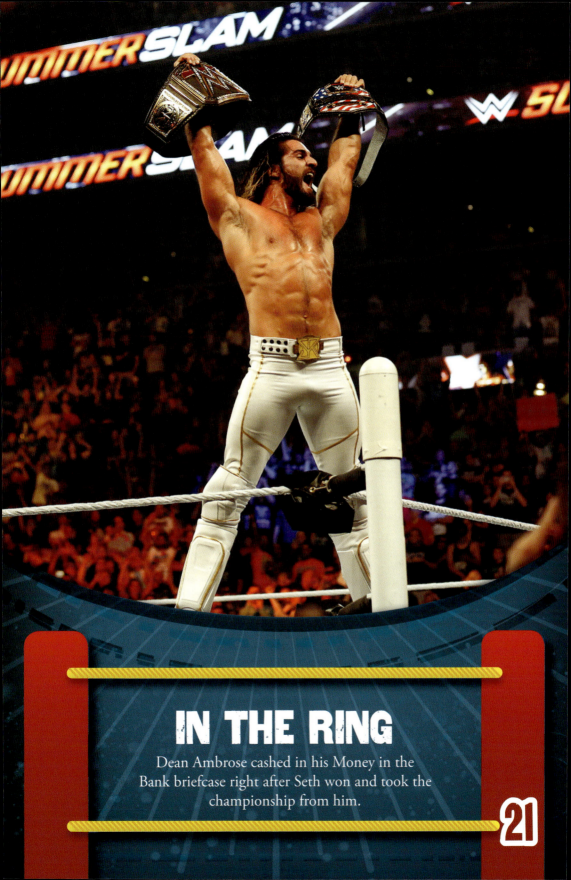

IN THE RING

Dean Ambrose cashed in his Money in the Bank briefcase right after Seth won and took the championship from him.

21

WRESTLEMANIA RUN

Seth was one of the top wrestlers in WWE at the end of 2016, even without the championship. He feuded with Triple H and faced "The Game" at WrestleMania 33 in 2017. Seth won the match using Triple H's own finisher, the pedigree!

IN THE RING

By SummerSlam 2017, Seth was working with Dean Ambrose as a tag team. They won the *Raw* Tag Team titles!

In October 2017, Seth and Dean joined back up with Roman Reigns, reforming The Shield for a short time. By April 2018, at WrestleMania 34, Seth was back on his own. He beat The Miz and Finn Bálor for the Intercontinental Championship!

IN THE RING

Seth is the first WWE wrestler to have held the NXT Championship, the WWE Championship, and the Universal Championship.

The year 2019 held more big moments for Seth. He won the 2019 Royal Rumble and a match against WWE Universal Champion Brock Lesnar. At WrestleMania 35, Seth and Brock opened the show. And Seth walked away the champ!

IN THE RING

Seth lost the title to Brock—and then won it back at SummerSlam 2019!

BROCK LESNAR

27

SETH'S FUTURE

Seth Rollins continued to be a top superstar into 2020. He joined forces with the Authors of Pain and Buddy Murphy. He fought Kevin Owens, but lost, at WrestleMania 36. What's next for Seth Rollins?

IN THE RING

In 2019, Seth got engaged to WWE superstar Becky Lynch. The couple had a baby in December 2020.

THE BEST OF SETH ROLLINS

SIGNATURE MOVES
the stomp, phoenix splash

FINISHERS
pedigree, ripcord knee

ACCOMPLISHMENTS
WWE Universal Champion, WWE World Champion, WWE Intercontinental Champion, WWE U.S. Champion, WWE Tag Team Champion, first-ever NXT Champion, ROH World Champion

MATCHES TO WATCH
Elimination Chamber 2014 vs. The Wyatt Family (with the Shield); Royal Rumble 2015 vs. John Cena vs. Brock Lesnar; Money in the Bank 2019 vs. A.J. Styles

FOR MORE INFORMATION

BOOKS

Abdo, Kenny. *Seth Rollins: The Architect*. Minneapolis, MN: Fly! An imprint of Abdo Zoom, 2020.

Black, Jake. *WWE Ultimate Superstar Guide*. New York, NY: DK | Penguin Random House, 2018.

WEBSITES

Seth Rollins | WWE
www.wwe.com/superstars/seth-rollins
Stay up to date with Seth's career on the official WWE website.

WWE Profile – Seth Rollins
www.espn.com/wwe/story/_/id/17165220/wwe-profile-page-seth-rollins
Find out more about Seth's accomplishments as a wrestler here.

Publisher's note to educators and parents: Our editors have carefully reviewed these websites to ensure that they are suitable for students. Many websites change frequently, however, and we cannot guarantee that a site's future contents will continue to meet our high standards of quality and educational value. Be advised that students should be closely supervised whenever they access the internet.

GLOSSARY

debut: to make a first appearance

developmental: having to do with the growth of something or someone

episode: a TV show that is part of a series

feud: a long fight between two people

independent: not owned by a larger business

main roster: in pro wrestling, a list of people who perform in the main shows or events

match: a contest between two or more people

stable: in pro wrestling, a group that often performs and competes together

tournament: a sports contest that many teams or people take part in over the course of many days

INDEX

Ambrose, Dean 12, 13, 17, 21, 23, 24
Bryan, Daniel 12
Cena, John 18
Florida Championship Wrestling (FCW) 8, 10
Iowa 4
Jacobs, Jimmy 8
Kane 12
Lesnar, Brock 18, 26, 27
Lynch, Becky 29
Mahal, Jinder 11
NXT 10, 11, 24
Orton, Randy 14
Reigns, Roman 12, 13, 15, 17, 18, 20, 24
Ring of Honor (ROH) 6, 8
Ryback 12
Sheamus 14
Shield, The 12, 13, 14, 16, 17, 24
Triple H 16, 17, 22
WrestleMania 14, 16, 18, 22, 24, 26, 28